THE TRUTH OF A NAKED SOUL

THE TRUTH OF A NAKED SOUL

A.T. Sahota

The Awakened Press

Copyright © 2019 by A.T. Sahota
All rights reserved.

Editing and Book Development Provided By
The Awakened Press
www.theawakenedpress.com

David Moratto, cover and interior design.

Sri Yantra By N. Manytchkine

This is a work of fiction, using well-known historical and public figures. Where real-life historical or public figures appear, the situations, incidents, and dialogues concerning these persons are entirely fictional and are not intended to change the entirely fictional nature of the work, and resemblance to persons living or dead is entirely coincidental.

No part of this publication may be reproduced, stored in a retrieval system, or transmitted in any form or by any means, electronic, mechanical, recording, or otherwise, without the prior written permission of the authors, except by a reviewer who wishes to quote brief passages in connection with a review written for inclusion in a print or online magazine, newspaper, periodical, blog, or broadcast.

First edition.

ISBN 978-1-989134-02-3

Dedicated to
BYT-DWD

Contents

ACT I		1
Chapter One	The Darkness	3
Chapter Two	Imperfection	15
Chapter Three	The Hunger	25
ACT II		39
Chapter Four	Tara	41
Chapter Five	Rumi	59
ACT III		75
Chapter Six	Relationship	77
Chapter Seven	Transformation	87
ACT IV		105
Chapter Eight	The End	107
	Epilogue	109
Chapter Nine	The Final Beginning	111

Words have power
Power has no words
—A.T.

ACT I

chapter one
The Darkness

Her face lingers in my memory—if only I had another day or night... tassels of hair cascading down her shoulder...childishly watching me as she sat—squatting on the toilet...I admired myself in the mirror...handsome, the pose of my youth... With my muscles, bodybuilder flex, sucking in my stomach...she would laugh at me...

It was either this scene or the taste of her pussy—not sure which one I like the best when I remember my time with her.

My heart aches in this memory... I never would do the right thing—what tradition calls for...the pining of my soul creates the drug I long for...

I remembered the night she asked if I would listen to her poetry.
    Nothing came further from my mind, that there would be magic in her words... I should have known—she has a way with reality...shifting space—when I wasn't careful it seeped into my brain...her magic was.... No, IS powerful.

Sometimes there would be an acute sense of sound rushing into my ears—blood through the veins and walls breathing...crickets in the night—I felt my own power in these moments,

    King Maker...that's what we call this kind of woman.

Can I go back?—or take back what was lost?...maybe she would find mercy for a deeply broken man...

Her poetry lingers... Not like the fragrance of perfume... A linger, like the taste of smokey old whiskey and a good cigar...

    Hmmm, who is the poet now my love?

Picasso. His raw charcoal on paper... distorted lines, created from the thoughts in his head... What he can do to a woman—now that I admire...

Perhaps Picasso's mind has similar thoughts. A dark beast lurks in the depths of my mind, screaming... "Those fucking whores will never get the best of me...not even the sweet taste of their passion or their face filled with fear in a deep, hard fuck..."

That night, as I lay on the bed, I could feel the words of her poetry enter my body—she didn't know then...it was the last time I would let my heart get the best of me. The words penetrated my soul...I was falling into a deep rich void.

    The simplicity struck me, and then I was lost...lost in the cadence of her pain, her anguish, and her power... I got lost in my own steaming jealousy and seduced by the mystery of transformation—I want to be King.

Her voice throwing me fast and further down an ancient hole—not even I dared to follow...

    Consumed by the tapestry of words, sparks of electric prose seemed to vibrate through my being. Spellbound, they took me

Sensing a scar of memories… Tara, Picasso and Rumi
    Maybe I have it backwards,
    An affair struck by my own pain
    A beast lurking in the shadows
    And the purity of innocence…
    She loved me… For all it's worth…

The Dark Beast

I have always known of a darkness
Not of his true nature,
But holding of a force only a God may contend with
I have a burning desire to come upon him
To go deep into the bowels of his own hell…
Awaken his slumbering demon,
Lay upon his breast and call to his silent passions
The thundering of a pain
Loosening its grip
Among the well placed locks
Its prison can no longer hold the bellows…
A cry rings out into the universe
Seething, the darkness crawls out from the abyss
Rupturing through its swollen canal,
Birthed into true form
Its terrifying power possessing
My tender soul
Its lust has no rules
Toying with the Gods is not a thing to do
Yet, I lay in my nakedness
My breath heavy with desire
My flower ripe with want
You have come for me
Brash in your manner,
Fully entrenched in your demonic passions
Cursing me for my purity
Never knowing
It will be the pure light of my heart that will quell the beast
You will take me,

Not knowing what will become, of you and I
Structures can no longer contain
the whipping storm that will crash and fill me
Distorting the lines of what they call love
And I, knowing this is what true love can hold
In the palm of truth and illusion
An awakened beast can sleep peacefully in my being

Your Walls

The pain and suffering
Of a wounded heart can tear at the soul of another
The crashing down of a well-laid wall
Can kill you if you are not careful
The emptiness that was left in the wake of betrayal
Is calling to my heart
I am caressed by your pain...
Wanting to mend its festering wound
Am I strong enough?
You ask, not in words but in your pushing me away
And I respond to the question...
My heart is gently bringing you in...
Slowly,
As to not disturb the wave of grief that needs release
I will hold you, forever...
If you will let me

The flow of an Invitation

My body is yearning and I am dripping…
A powerful fantasy fills my being
My life force quickens
Beating a reminder into my chest
I have wanted you for an eternity.
A sensing of excitement grabs a wave into my heart
I am riding on the lust of your wanting
A gentle finger on my flowered awakening
The flow of an invitation
And your body now hardens
In a fast knowing…
"She desires for me to take her"
The innocence within the core
Pushes out an intense need
To pull you in…
With a reminder of all that's exposed in surrender.
The heat of your breath finds its place on my neck
Speaking loudly a gust of desire
I feel you pressing into me
And my body again crying into a deep wanting
Your hands finding their way across the landscape of my being
Your arousal now searching for its home…
Finding it through a wanting grind…
Slipping into its rightful place
My body taking you in
A soft tightening and quickening
And I am filled
A sensation rushing through my core
Screaming in ecstasy the cells vibrate and dance

Thrusting deeply, a surge of power, releases an explosion that your whole body responds to

And I, a moist gush of intensity flowing along your body…
You kiss me, deep and long
Intimate in its connection and gratitude for the complete surrender

Dark Things

We first manifest the unspoken, the dark things that hide deep
 within the bowels of our being
Unwilling to see these aspects of ourselves
Because we are broken
Too much pain has come to pass
an unruly personality
With desperate desires to destroy
Unwilling, to see the Truth… it is I who creates all realities…
Behaviors unspoken, blinding
One must take a dive into
Illumination to find the reasons why
Blistering cold reality
Lies and betrayal of the true self
What is found hiding among the foggy depths
Innocent child…

Deep in My Soul

There is an empty place in my soul…
It is heavy and it burns…
Crying to be touched and fed,
Passion wells up inside me, wanting its release…
Aching with a longing so deep…
Seeking a connection to my soul
When will he be ready to recognize me?
Or has he already, and I am too scared to take him in
The passing moments, only a glimpse of my longing
Reminding me of the emptiness
That burns deep into my soul

To The Ancient King

My love, I have returned from my slumber,
Ancient and wise
Golden Light once again will flow through your veins
Mighty as a king, fierce as the jaguar
Tell me your sorrows deeply held in the chambers of your heart
What did the Red Queen say as she struck you down, beneath her feet?
The volcano now awakens, the rumble of fiery passion, no longer
    contained…
"Come to me"
Bellows burning… Quickening arises a silent strength
The flush of hunger, to soar once again
Beats a rhythm of knowing…
A legend ignites
I am here to whisper Truth into your being
And that whisper becomes a full breath of longing
Guiding a way
The stars have spoke of this coming age
Triumphant is your return
Embracing a moment of glory
To witness the Grace of a new world

Chapter Two

Imperfection

Somewhere deep in our psyche
There is a core belief that we are unlovable...
The abandoned child within has been wounded.
Lack of self-love has sprouted,
It grows like a fierce weed
of hate and violence towards self and our neighbor
—TARA

My own imperfections get the best of me, when I'm not looking.
The world can create a beast in a man.
Like it or not, this is the truth.
    The Mind beats the shit out of me most of the time. It's a never-ending battle

How she did it, I do not know—I want it from her... Waiting for a chance to take it the ease and grace. No fear walking into a room, the friendly smile that draws people close. She can see them. The truth of their soul, she knows them so deeply. How can a person make another feel as though they were the only one in the world?

I want her power; she will never do anything with it.

I can wield it, mold my own destiny. She cannot see what she has.

Tara tells me she works for God. I believe she does, or is she God herself?

Quantum Entangle

Quantum entangle
Twists my fate
And struggle sets its illusionary path of entrapment
For it is only my pain and wanting choice that keeps me locked into
    the suffering,
my beloved pain…
What does it take to unlock this bitter war, the fight against my
    own being
Believing there is no chance for happiness
Silence as I sit in stillness
Awareness catches the truth…
And I wait, slow in a decision
Truth in a choice
As I sink into the cold depths of
despair,
Surrender begins to emerge
Freedom comes to the tethers that bind
I begin to relax
And then it comes, freedom
Born from the murky depths of my being
I simply float to the surface
No longer bound by a forced illusion
The choice of letting go
For one true breath in bliss

No One Here

Writhing through my body
Pusing little pools of skin
An intensity of burning hate
Pours out through my being
And I am laid out, unable to move
In this victimless world
No one to come hold me as the pain begins to ooze down my legs
Where is everyone?... Oh wait there is no one here but me
Caught in my own illusion of self hatred
The mother's breast was not offered to me when I was born
And now God calls to me... "Wake up from your slumber"...   Go
    out and love a forgotten world
I sit here saying "What the fuck!!" ... Who am I to do this work
I can only pretend for so long... Can you read the signs, as I push
    away everything that comes onto my path?
I fucking hate this shit—because I sit here alone... Not one person
    to come and rescue me
Oh wait! This is how I created it... To keep the story alive
I can say I am hugely successful at being alone and pushing love
    away
Nothing left to do, death is not here yet
It's what I truly long for... Death
I will take either, the physical death
or
the death of what keeps me
from being loved

The Unsheltered Heart

Washed away in an ocean of oblivion
Searching for the tossed weight of another soul
I find you, alone in the distance
On a shore turned to ruin
There is no pain here
Only the heartbeat of an unforgiving wreck
And I cry in the wake of such loneliness
The opening of a portal…
Long forgotten in time
Churning into darkness
lost in grief
The waves conquer what has become shaken at its core
You decide in your own time what will be forgiven and what will
 remain untouched
I will temper the storm within my own being,
Awaiting the return of an unsheltered heart
Beating out a rhythm, awakened to its truth
You cannot hide forever
She will find you… That kiss

Our Limitations

Why do we fall asleep in our own limitations?
Fattening into a bulge of despair
Did you really think that you would be given the option of
    hopelessness?
Ingrained in your patterns, never breaking free
And what is all that freedom dancing around you?
What a loathsome annoyance of your own envy
Unable to feel the bliss while peeking through the window of
    another's existence
Your only passion is to shield your own light
The weight of your belief crushing every beat of your heart
Punishing the thought of a breath towards happiness
And you say God is to blame, for it is He who holds you in
    compliance and
A veiling, deepening the numbing of your own brilliance
You walk a dark path, following the footsteps of your own
    persecution
Shaken into oneness of absolution and pity
Never knowing your own freedom

Untitled

Tonight I hold a truth
Set before me... I crumble
All illusion is set free
I am wrecked in a memory of a love I have betrayed
Only in words, yet the words hold great power
My heart broken
For my mind speaks of fear and separation
I, as a woman, know better...
and though the words still come.
They are not the truth of my heart
And he reads them
Now my love, he hides from me
I cannot hold him in my arms and tell him the truth
He will no longer listen
I lay alone

Illusions

The prison of Time and Space
Build walls out of Illusions
Throughout the mind
Ticking of the clock holds its weight down around you
Separating you from the truth
Lies seek to destroy that which has brought you from formless to form
Is this just a game?
Can you find your way through the shattered fear...
and untold images?
Those that float through the tempered field
Who is the one who holds the key to free you from this loathsome trap?
Equal in its unbinding torment
You seek answers only to find there are none
Cold in the bitter reality,
It sinks into your form
Illusion is just a fairy tale
And the awakened one,
A dream, to hold close to the heart
There is no committed piece of this fabric that truly holds you here
Only the withering justification
Of an old story
Finding its way to bind you in its own game of illusions
To break free you must find the strength
The Knowing
The illusion has been your choice all along

My Wings

My wings are the color of a Rainbow
Shimmery iridescent magic
Wondering how to hold you… They become black as night,
Glossy with strength
As they spread their power
To fend off the unwanted stranger
The majestic space of my wings takes the form of your Divinity
To remind you that your Greatness far exceeds your deepest desires…
And you know the secrets that lay
In the folds of your own heart.
If only you remembered, you have your own wings…
In the embrace of soaring ecstasy,
wings always sing on the whisper of your Truth

The Random Nature of Imperfection

Who are we to think differently?
Distortions of reality dig a grave of illusion
And I want something different
Chaos and bursts of uncertainty
Caressing a possibility of the impossible
And a battle is breaking through.
No one tells you to fight for your existence
Fight for a dream that calls out to you,
From a distant shore
The hump and grind form a chain around our imagination
Trying to save us from breaking all the rules
And the Random Nature of Imperfection is taunting me as I
    surrender into its simplicity
Floating on freedom that I call my own
For a moment a release out of the mold
And I became lost in the pureness of truth
There is something Divinely perfect in imperfection
A secret only a few can share, with eyes to see

Chapter Three

The Hunger

There is something otherworldly about a woman who has touched her own power. My hunger and her wanting clash together, I love this game. So many fantasies fill me, each woman and each dream a game I play to fill my time. Maybe giving me the charge I need to fuel my ambition. It is late and the office has cleared for the day. My boredom getting the best of me tonight. I have a long report to complete.

I can feel it in her loins, the pulsing, pulling sensation.

Her wanting and longing pulling at my soul.

I lay in my office, the white leather couch cold on my skin, all of the blood has left my head. My heart is racing as I reach for my cock. I look up at the Picasso drawing on the wall, a reminder of what I search for. Shuddering from the imagined thrusting, I am stunned that I still cry with the release.

My Yearning

The power that comes from my desire and longing can move mountains…
It is what turns the Earth and breaks a sapling free from its seed…
You feel it when I call to you..
That pulling sensation…
That is the claim of a woman,
My yearning, longing and desire
The searing hot need for your hard cock to take me…
My pussy dripping in longing…
Sending out a signal…
Desire is a moist passionate sensation that shifts consciousness…
Heightening awareness of the world around you —
I have the power to shift you into altered states of being,
God flows through me. Effortless. Like a river moving down a mountain…
I give this to you because I deem you worthy of great potential…
We both rise to the occasion to meet God

Nectar of the Gods

Nectar of the Gods with
A rush of ecstasy
A fleeting rise of your glorious body
And I, a God in all my right
To take upon myself, a pleasure that runs so deep
One so fair to drip an everlasting love
My passion burns into your soul
Releasing desire to bring you closer,
yet you are the greatest of mysteries
Slipping through the veils of possession and wrapping into my
    heart,
Its true home
I call to you
You return with endless wonder
In a wave of relief,
It is I, lost and rewarded for conquest to be held
I AM forever in service to a Divine cause
Rapture into a true desire of Oneness
And with a searing into my soul,
"I still remember just the way you taste"

Untitled

Time Stands still at the thought of your touch
Softly you reach into the folds of my being
The sweetness of passion cries into a wetness of desire
A wave of ecstasy shoots through my body
I surrender into the moment
Two bodies moving,
Hot and breathless in wonder
I call to you…
The nectar of the Goddess guides you in
Deep into my pleasure
I envelop you
My desire now tightly wrapped around you,
I crash on the shores of your wanting
The release of rapture…
Moves me through your soul

Passion

Silently I sit waiting
As my body raptures into an ecstasy
Beyond words
Form can no longer hold the waves of passion exploding from wanting
An illusion cresting in breath
My heart a pounding force
I imagine your touch,
Gentle and warm…
There is a familiarity in this place
Caressing deepens into surrender
Of all that was known before
my breath can no longer grab for anything but you
The surge of energy rises
my body whispers louder and louder…
Take me

My Pain

My pain comes in layers
Awareness floats beyond the walled prison
And I shall no more say this is my truth
Beyond the layers of confusion there is a gift held so tightly with desire
You have returned unto me...
My thoughts have strayed to illusions past,
now I see my truth lay before me
Still waters deeply caressed by waves of passion
Rising in a heat filled plume, you dive deep into my heart
I am caught by waves of emotion so powerful I sway, trance like...
Grace becomes the fuel of my cellular form and I no longer exist
It is you who stirs the depths of my soul
it is you who lay upon my breast the finite caress that strengthens
    my being
I no longer walk alone

Meeting

The rise and fall of my breath envelops my whole being
Surrender can come if I wasn't shaking with wonder
I can hear him now… Senses reaching out, through a blindfold
The only true way is to be silent
and listen to the energy…
He meets me… My heart a vibration of two energies as one…
I no longer know the difference
How I long for his touch
To fulfill a fantasy, months in the making
My heart is crying now,
wonder can be a sad song
Unsure, even after all the preparation
His breath… first to touch my skin
Warm soft hands reach to my check,
His Knowing strong
his lips, the only voice I will hear…
Find their way to meet mine
My heart finds its way
Through that kiss

The Meeting

I can sense your vibration as you enter the room
Heart beating fast in response to anticipation
As you move closer, your scent touches me
Desire and fear ignite a stirring within
You step closer… slowly
I am trembling now, blinded by fabric
My anticipation grows stronger
As you reach for my body
Intense vibration stills my longing
Hot breath pressing on my lips
There is a pause…
the silence becomes loud
Searing rush of adrenaline seeps into my being
Connection pulls you in
Our lips awakening the memory of two souls
Even quicker the beat of my heart
Becomes the swirling of energies
I melt into you with desire

Melting Inhibitions

I take you into my warm soft mouth
A rhythm of ecstasy unleashes a great wanting
More of me responds with
A grid against your body
Every cell an exploding nucleus,
Senses heightened… electric sparks
My body aches for you to take me
Eyes meet, inviting you into my being
Surrender comes to me in your touch,
Melting all my inhibitions
The breath, a whisper of deeper intentions
Filling me with a way undiscovered
Swollen with desire the yearning leads you
Dripping from a knowing of pleasure,
Pleading for you to enter my sacred portal
Nectar releasing,
A Divine flow guides you deep into me
Passion tightens, pulling you into oneness
The pulsing quickens
As you receive pleasure,
I am a river
My force crashing onto your rock
Hot, wet and gushing

Lust

My lust and my wanting
Make it so hard to breathe
I can feel you taking me
Energetic waves of passion
Yet your body is nowhere to be found
I am in rapture, this moment in ecstasy dancing through the nature
 of my being
Rapid beats of my heart swell my tender flower
I lay in stillness not wanting to miss this moment
I can feel you,
There are no boundaries and the longing has deepened into my core
It is only space that is the illusion
My soul pulls you closer as the rushes of intense heat and prickling
 sensations scream out in pleasure
The force of your being crashing into mine
In a knowing that there is only One
The pressure on my heart leaves it difficult to breathe again
The waves of sensation create a force… too dizzy to stand
I remember the kiss…
French restaurant on my birthday…

The Trust of One

Whispering on the truth
My body shivers like a memory that is not yet a dream
Lips touch and the breath becomes a wave across a titled ocean
Quivering in want
A sacred spark in an ecstatic dance
Pressing into a glorified vision
Hearts beating a rhythm to embrace what was lost in time
The Kiss is only the first step in a long awaited poem
Waiting seems like an eternity
The breath again draws us in like a fevered awakening,
Trembling in thought
Heart, breaking open, speaks of surrender
Fear tears open the wounds of the past
Lust can take hold if we melt into a trust of one
Our eyes meet in a knowing that pulls with the tides
Cresting into oblivion
That long awaited, "Yes"
fills every cell with an explosion of passion
Our bodies meet in a singular vibration
The pendulum swings into balance
Weaving into place an everlasting embrace
Thrust amongst the shore
Abandoned forever
Is the pain of loneliness.

ACT II

Chapter Four

Tara

THOUGHTS BY TARA—

Deep in the water there is something
so profound, stillness takes your breath away
and Grace holds you into surrender...
Sept. 2, 2012

The Prophecy

I was shaking that day, I remember it well
It was as if my cellular body knew the Matrix of my Destiny would
    be revealed
And the words would carry a weight into the records of my existence
Funny how I can remember every detail of when she walked
    through the door
My mind told me "don't be silly, you are just a nervous 16 year old"
    it was after all, my party.
A gift from my new stepmother, a welcoming into my new life…
I so yearned for a mother who would love me, and do all the things
    a mother and daughter would do together.
My Cinderella story…would continue, she just had a different face…
Would my friends show up? Shit! I can't remember all of my
    relatives' names….
The Fortune Teller… She stared right through my soul.
Could She read my mind?
Did She know I touched myself in secret places, a young girl should
    not know of?
Funny what we think inside of ourselves…
She smiled, and a warmth came over me, she walked to me…
With a knowing in her smile,
"Don't worry, it will be okay"…
Reliving this moment, She knew. She recognized me…just like I
    can recognize them now. The Awakened Ones.
I followed the laughter of the room; there was no one there to
    recognize the Matrix of Truth in those tender tealeaves.
In those moments of laughter and disbelief, I started to believe the
    same lie, as she read the future of everyone in the room.
Then she came to me, The Birthday Girl.

A hush fell over the room, and my heart began to pound, the same beat that started when she entered the party.
Quieting my body, so that it may sit in a memory of timelessness...
She spoke the prophecy...the minds of the audience, strangely silent with a few nervous laughter, to fill the awkwardness...
"You will have 5 children, but the last 2 will be the most important to you"
My mind racing, as if she was speaking the truth, "5 kids!"—That is way too much. Nervous laughter...
"You will have a career in the health profession, a doctor, nurse—healing arts."
Interesting—at one time I wanted to be a nurse—would have liked doctor, but my life did not support that path... That I knew.
You will get married, I see bright lights flashing, an Actor? Maybe a Fireman, All I see are lights, a policeman?
"You will live in a large house, it has a lot of windows"
The tealeaves, how do they show her pictures?
"The marriage will end when you are 45."
Oh that's so sad...
"After 47 you will meet your true love and be together."
Oh! Well that's good, but why so late in life and why wouldn't the first husband be my true love...doesn't sound like something I would do...
Dismissing the truth is so easy, when we are taught not to believe.
Everyone laughed and clapped... What a fun game.
I know there is more, more about Him, my true love... But the memory gets so foggy...
Time wanting her own way to present the information...
Maybe she is just as excited for the prophecy to come...
Years later, going through my life, an event will become the words she spoke that day... My Divorce emancipated in all its glory
Whisperings of the truth, in the cradle of a memory
Sometimes that truth will speak loudly, remembering what she said
Wake up Tara, it's going to happen, just wait...
Like you have learned to do!

Your Destiny is already etched into a path, clearly marked
Just walk and learn along the way
We will do the rest… Remember the first message
"Have faith and believe, no matter how despairing it looks"
My 47th birthday is up the road.
A quickening began at 45, without a memory of words gone by.
Does it really work this way? Or was She sent to me, by design, so I would understand that I was held tightly into the heart of the Divine?
Does one really just have to patiently wait?
Is Destiny already planned?
Is Fate just a dream that floats on the milky shores of life?
Who are we to really know the Matrix of Truth that guides us…
When we are too busy laughing at our powerful humanness?
The Ancient Ones called it "The Time Returns", the union of 2 physical beings,
One Soul
Coming together to fulfill a prophecy
True Love…
Not many will know it in this lifetime…
The searching becomes a painful reminder that they are alone…
Stepping through the pain, the path becomes brighter
He is there on the other side waiting for me…I just Believe.

Mother's Day

You sent me a text today
"Happy Mother's Day"
A seemingly quaint little text
Did you send it to your lawyer?
Or did you file it away with the love letters you stole from me?
Or is it you, that is happy I no longer play the role of mother in your children's lives
Erasing any guilt and shame that was your position since the day they were born
Does it still anger you that I loved them so deeply
Does your inner child still scream for his beloved mother's breast
While you lay awake watching your child feed from my bosom
Or was this passionate jealousy sprung upon you in the silent screams of your own nightmare
Did your pain awaken as my body pushed out an innocent life wanting to be loved?
My darling, I have loved you beyond the love of a child and yet you weep as though you have been pushed aside
In my own arrogance I was veiled of your truth
Deafened to you screams, by my own fears of intimacy...
Blinded from my own power...
Fears of not having enough within my own being
I never knew my own strength
until I lost you all

Lost Love

I lay caution to the wind…
While my heart dances over the wintery grave of another lost love
One dying is never going to get any easier
I lay awake wondering when this will all end…
I whisper to myself,
"Don't worry there will be another, and once again you will dance"
But what is it that we are dancing for?
Do we dare to dream that a love can exist?
…Or is it just a dream to keep us in hope and desire
Always reaching for the next drifting heart
Wondering again…
Is this the love I have been searching for?

God called me today...

I didn't want to answer
Tied to the delusion of love gone astray
Broken in my heart and ripped deep in my soul
Alone
Today is not a good day for me,
Tomorrow will not be better
Wishing the ringing would stop
Noise slicing through my tender nerves
"Ring, ring…ring, ring"
Not an ounce of me can move past this
Does God want to tell me what the others have already spoken
I have no idea about right and wrong anymore
I thought he was the one… the path so clear
Love in all its glory sweeping me into ecstasy… deep surrender into
    a false heart?
Is that even possible?
God, everyday you show me love—in all its forms
Fat, ugly, sexy, fun, and eternal
Yet for me…abandonment
I no longer choose to live

A Lie Told

My mind tries to define you
Wrapping existence into a package of perfection
Disappointment wanting to take its rightful place
Whispering an old truth.
"You will never have what you desire."
So I obey the lie I told myself years ago
Wanting something of liberation from an old pattern
Is it old or is it just the way?
I silence myself knowing that the Lie can be resolved
If I just let my heart lead
I come to the edge of the void
Terrified,
With the realization
It has been me all along
The holding back,
The wanting to know the lie
It is I now who has the choice
I can choose love
Not beholden to another's choices
Just to know that…
I am the choice
I am the freedom
I am the creator of my heart

Love is My God

Love is my God
Surrender is my pain
Illusion is my prison
Freedom is my choice

Love Me

Love me and I will unfold like a lotus…
Hold me and my will is yours
Honor me and I will worship your very essence
Make my passion burn into every cell of my body
I will take you into me
Dripping with want, tighten with desire
I will not let you go

My secret knowing

I have hid from the world for so long
Trapped in the illusions of non-comprehension
I have been lost in my own lack of surety
Not wanting to take a stand
In my own truth
Terrified no one will accept me as Divine Source...
This courses through my being
When I am alone, I feel it
My secret knowing...I keep to myself
The disappointment and frustration of my inability to be understood
I am a magical gift wanting to be opened
Yet I made the wrapping untouchable and the knots too tight
I put the gift in bulletproof glass with the security of the National Museum
This is the challenge I give to any suitor...
I'm looking for the bravest, strongest and wisest warrior to herald the call and carry through the task
Why??
I want to shine as I am, stand in my truth... Share my knowledge and wisdom...
Show others their magic
No need to hide...
I found this in my wisdom...
No need to protect my heart...
There is freedom in this

Humanity

It came upon me today, the feeling I hold in my heart for Humanity…
For they are like small children, needing to be held, loved and forgiven…
Humanity is but a young race in the presence of the universe.
Patience is stirring and the knowing that humanity in all of its abilities to love and evolve, is what drives me to this expansion in my heart,
A deep presence of unconditional love…
It's coming, the peace, the abundance, the Grace…

Letting Go

Feel like I've been gone a lifetime,
Not remembering the torn pieces of my past
What does it take to shatter your dreams?
So the new ones can be born
At last…
Silence is stunning, when basking in its own power

The sea has filled me with the song of the Siren…
She calls to me that I am home…
Baptized in the waters of passion,
I let go

Sailor

I fell in love with a sailor,
I fell in love with the sea…
Pining away for something that could never be.
And then I wished on a star
Upon a light so bright
They brought my true love to me
on that very night
Now I lay upon the sea
Wrapped into the mystery
Of Heaven's love and fairy tales
And Happiness amongst the whales
Wishing on the starry night
For my love to hold me in passion's embrace…
Entwined in the magic of his soft kisses upon my face.
Secrets to be held
Magic fills a deep hole
Longing for my beloved to caress my soul

Mermaid Poem

I was a mermaid in the sea
And you were there, just you and me
Filling our days with sunshiny bliss
And under the stars we did kiss
Our love is traveling through all time
Lasting forever our hearts intertwined
Now we meet once again
Our passion burns
There is no end
Though we find ourselves apart
The connection just deepens into one heart
And now you are a sailor on the sea and I am on land looking for thee
I will look to the stars and find you there,
knowing there is no time and space for what we share
Though our lives may once again drift us apart
All it takes is a connection deep into the heart
That is were we will find that intense passion
And once again our hearts will be
entwined in connection

Morning Promise

Morning whispers of promise
Tears of joy flowing through my heart
Wonder beats a song pulsing through the body
I am grateful for my connections
We speak sometimes of emptiness
Not realizing the illusion was an ancient choice
Awakening mends the split and once again
The dance of the beloveds
Rises up through the mists of time
Feeling the embrace as it warms my face and feeds my soul

Desire

I am standing at the edge of my Desire
Looking down upon it...
Unable to fully grasp the depth of longing that has pulled me to
    this place...
A distant memory of a walk I took...
Never knowing how one moment can forever change a life...
I am standing here...a distant 500 miles away...the vision again
    pulling me back to that place...
My vision holds a precious memory...
The way he looked at me—I felt him, his entire being declaring
    his love for me...and this time on this land, I knew its
    truth...and I knew in that moment how deeply I loved him...
I stand here, embarking on a journey, this place already my
    home...
Now to manifest all of it in the physical...
Desire
    —Sedona 2016

Chapter Five

Rumi

My Divine

Seek and ye shall find me
Touch me and I shall be your presence
Ask me and I shall guide you through the murky waters of your
    perceptions
My heart is awakened and there is no need to have fear
I am a wave of thought followed by a feeling
I will come through you…
Only to send your brilliance along its path
Forsaken you are not
Held and you are Holy
Love shall ever be abundant in my place
Doubt will have no want
And my heart is yours for the taking

Rumi

They say that when Rumi met Shams of Tabriz, it was an instantaneous recognition, and a knowing of what was to come.
As if the soul knew all the answers, like the body knows to breathe.
They walked away from the world, 40 days and 40 nights…
That's all it took to find the entrance into the heart of God.
Easy was the path because Shams had The Way.
Maybe it was easier back then. In ancient times people still believed in God.
Humans were simpler, less technology to answer questions of nature.
Rumi was never the same. The union was between two people, yet it was always about the Absolute Truth. One can never imagine how you can find God through the eyes of a stranger. To know the bliss of that discovery, one must allow Grace.
Rumi and Shams had that. Sometimes we get lucky and we can awaken to Truth through the open heart of Love.
Maybe we do not think it's possible. The heart becomes cold and hard, through the experiences of life. Forgotten and misrepresented, is what becomes of the path.
Everyone is longing for connection and searching for anything that will dull the pain. Mostly distracted by survival, media or drama. Who is to say when it will end. Awakening is not for the faint of heart, a warrior's path, only because you must break down all the walls and barriers to find the Truth.
Once I met a man, I met God in his eyes and thought it was love.
It was only my reflection.

Grace

Something opens our wings
Something makes boredom and hurt disappear
Someone fills the cup in front of us
We taste only grace...

—Rumi

Embrace by the Moon...

I am Raw in the stillness
My heart caressing a wave of grief...
That lies can only dream to become.
And who Am I in this silky darkness you call the void?
Where time stands still...
Awaiting an embrace by the
Moon...
Pulling at emotions buried so deep they have no name...
I stand alone in my innocence facing a truth...
The hunger of Oneness taints my breath and whispers to my
    flowering passion...
"Wait for he will find you"
I can only imagine what he will feel like...
His hard body pressing against my sweetness of life.
His breath hot with a need to fill me,
We become one in desire...
A poetic geometry surrounds us,
As our eyes meet with Knowing...
Oneness seeps into our being and the prophecy is fulfilled

Not Forgotten

Awakening to the budding of a new existence
What lies beneath the surface is yet undiscovered
Passions meet encountered by another time,
I sit by your side
Held between the worlds
Traversing a sometimes painful way
And you reach out to me
With a heart bleeding from another love
Sparked by wonder and yet still trapped incomplete
Seeking a way to right a wrong
Only to find its wholeness in the arms of an embrace
Eyes have yet to tell the tale of the soul
Trust, an unwavering truth if it is allowed in
By the grace of the gift
We walk together
Dripping in knowing of illusions rendered
Pretenses lost in a stream pulled down,
Washed into oblivion
The light of a holy one brightens in response
To a dream that has not been forgotten

Untitled

I come to you naked in my devotion
Raw in the knowing of my heart
Neither material, nor spiritual possessions will bind us
For this love goes beyond the needs of any tether
I come fully exposed, my heart has wept its final stagnation
Only the purest of love steps forth in an offering
Come to me, so that love envelops the wisdom that has come from time
There are no vows or contracts that must be honored
Nor among the material realm wrapping its web around us
This love, deeper than the abyss
Stronger than the mystical light that binds
Pure in a knowing I love you from the core of my being, unrestrained…

Holy Union

I put a call out to the universe today
I am ready for The Change
I am ready to walk a path so deep I tremor with honor at its existence
I know not where this journey will take me
I only know that my "yes" pulls me into belonging
Diving into the depths of my deepest darkness
To stay in connection when all I want to do is run
In this decision…in total stillness, I call to my Beloved
Come dance with me, allowing freedom in this place to sweep us off our feet
Walk with me on a path blinded in unconditional love
And bask with me in the return of the greatest flame contained in our presence
Filled with a sense of wonder and awe
Only God will shine through the spark of an embrace
As we rest into
Holy Union

The Kiss

And my heart finds its way
To you
Through that kiss

Awakening to The Twin Flame

Edge to edge a gentleness forms into connection
And what lay before them is
A path unclear
Opportunity like this comes once in an eternity
The lessons beholden can pull it all back
Waves of ecstasy burn into a lover's soul
To deny the Great Gift will set a spin into oblivion
Who so dares to merge into Oneness?
Delights in a path complete
Rivers flow and shape a boundless
Cause
Reaching far back into time
When it all began
Core to core an explosion of essence
And the first born of its kind,
Masters a different realm
Union between two souls
The path is awakened

Make love to me

Make love to me…
as the notes hit my body in a shimmery dance…exciting my skin…
Make love to me…
as your excitement rises and the Matisse moves the heat of desire
Make Love to me…
biting my flesh as I melt into deep surrender
Make love to me…
as my body opens from a depth so great, I gush in ecstasy
Make love to me…
looking into my soul as God awakens in our being
Make love to me…
as a flame births into the universe, igniting Power and Grace
Make love to me…
because your soul belongs in mine
Make love to me…
because my soul belongs in you

Divine love

You are my Infinite Love, my Holy of Holies,
my Divine manifest in physical form…
I breathe you in as God incarnate
I inhale your magnificence into my being,
igniting the passion of the infinite within…
My Beloved, I caress your sweetness of Divine incantation,
My mouth dripping in Holy Kisses to awaken your Truth…
My heart sees only your exquisite splendor of 1000 Kings laid upon
    your breast…beholden to your Light

The Journey Back to Twin Flame

As I touch your quivering skin,
My eyes look deep into your soul...
To call you home,
My beloved...
Our journey has been long
With time pressed into the folds of space
Separation makes us yearn,
With only the knowing of a union to come when all has been complete.
Experiences of lesson lingering,
to show us gratitude in the Divine Union.
The path of awakening can be the length of eternity...
I wonder, where have you been?
Who did you love?
And who has loved you?
Has time played a soft song as you sailed along her shores?
What filled your heart with passion?
And what made you weep the tears of grief so great...
Was your greatest lesson learned through sacrifice?
Did you ride the waves of expansion with courage?
And did your contraction help you to explore the depths of your being...
Searching for who you are...
Essence touching its own brilliance while we wait for The Time Returns...
To share in the joy of coming home...
And bask in the glory of the journey
To remind us,
Existence seeks to fill the silence
Truth can only be won from the walk through time...
And the quiver is only the recognition
Of me within you.

Oneness

You move me into stillness
Resting in Your arms
Motionless tides of Oneness
Merging together
One breath, One wave, One Being
Ecstasy dancing in creation…
Finding the rhythm and comfort
As Home

ACT III

Chapter Six
Relationship

There are Horizontal and Vertical relationships.

A Horizontal Relationship is the relationship that never goes anywhere. There is no growth, no movement. There is no transformation and liberation from pain and suffering. Patterns are repeated. Time moves still. Happiness is eluded. Opportunity for growth is abundant, yet no one seeks to claim the advantages of the true purpose of relationship.

To Wake Up.

All relationships are formed for wake up. No matter if they are friendship, romantic, or family. What we seek is a path of healing and transformation. To end the shut off heart, the pains of hurt and the pains of suffering. One seeks connection, heart fully open embracing the gift of true happiness. The result of this growth is connection. Finding Oneness is the destination to God. This is the Vertical relationship.

The Vertical relationship is where the wake up, the illumination of patterns that create separation are revealed. One becomes awakened to the habitual beliefs and behaviors that keep the heart shut down.

Where the pain and suffering are triggered once again, this time willing to be released. To get free from what keeps one disconnected.

The Vertical relationship, with velocity, takes one to God, the Divine Source, where through the open heart two can become one. The ultimate connection.

Yet, what happens in this relationship is the emotional triggers and charges that are set off as time bombs when relating to one another, cause the hurt one to retreat into the cave of isolation.

The other partner in turn seeks to justify the behavior with frustration and anger, thus shutting down the heart and ceasing to find compassion and unconditional love.

I have related in this way my whole life. Even in romantic relationships where I could swear my heart is wide open. I am smacked in the face by an unconscious gesture, an invisible force closing my heart. I'm in lock down.

The last time this happened, the wreckage and damage was so great my partner, wounded from the blow, left for good. It was inevitable at the velocity I was going down.

My question became, "If I was so sure that I wanted the Vertical relationship with this man, where did I go wrong?"

Maybe I didn't. As I looked at my behaviors, my patterns during this relationship I noticed something. My wake up was happening. Never in a relationship was I so aware of my fear of losing love, my fear of connection and my vulnerability. Never had I pushed someone away so hard. Every time my heart opened and I exposed my love, chaos ensued.

My friends thought it wasn't healthy, yet I was finding my voice. I had been deeply looking at the "hows" and the "whys" I shut my heart off. I was growing, even when it looked and felt messy. It was a vertical path of growth.

My partner thought I was crazy. A turned on, hyper volatile woman. Hot and cold, on and off. Heart open and closed. I continued with my practices and meditations. I stayed connected even at the worst of times. And I found my heart. I reached into my most vulnerable places and spoke. I would then turn around and shut off.

We were monogamous in our relationship. The energy between us intensified and I became terrified I would lose him.

I began my research on relationships. I happened upon a teacher who spoke of the Vertical relationship, monogamy and something I never heard of and did not quite understand, "The claiming of a man."

She speaks about the roles in relationship between a man and a woman. The woman has the ability of call and response and the man is a responder. From my perspective I began to understand that a woman puts out a call to find her partner and the man responds to that call.

Sounds simple, yet when a woman has a man, finds her partner why do they not stay?

My teacher would go on to speak about claiming a man. The woman must do this.

Here is the secret. Ladies, listen carefully. A man becomes wobbly in the relationship because the woman becomes wobbly. When the woman has fear, shuts down, pushes away, has thoughts that this man of hers cannot hold her, doesn't love her, etc. the man becomes wobbly and becomes available to another call. In this case he seeks another woman.

It's a woman's steadfast claim that this man is the one that will keep the man from the arms of another woman.

And it goes deeper. What is the man searching for? What are men truly looking for in a woman, the right woman, the woman who has the ability to claim them? A woman who will end the roaming….the hunting that feels like the endless game of men.

Men are searching for a powerful woman that they can trust with their deepest of secrets….their wounding.

Man, through time have been the protectors, the hunters, and the warriors of the tribe.

A man must face all the dangers to provide for his tribe. And how is that accomplished?

Men have a fascinating game they play amongst themselves. Since the dawn of time men have gathered together in a kinship of creating strong men. As boys, they tease each other, play games to outwit and overcome the other in battles of strength. They wrestle, chase, climb trees, make forts, and push each other's buttons. This is the most primal games, survival of the fittest.

If a boy begins to show signs of weakness the other boys of the tribe gather together, pick on him to make him stronger. It would be a dangerous place to show his fellow tribe mates a man has feelings and emotions. That the verbal jab hurt, or the wrestling match scared him. The tribe is only as strong as its weakest link.

While women gather in circles, bonding through sharing their deepest emotions, through touch, tears and love. The men are basically beating the warrior into each other.

Seems primitive and yet these rituals are so ingrained into our primal DNA codes that we are on automatic.

As women we also understand what it takes to hold, nurture and love anyone who is in pain. This is our birthright.

What a man seeks is a woman who can hold the place where his heart has been wounded every time he was in battle.

When you claim a man you are not stating that he belongs to you, that no other woman has the rights to him, or the man has obligation of monogamy with you.

A woman cannot use her persuasive powers of feminine lure and beauty to claim a man. A _true claim_ of a man is a powerful commitment to hold a sacred place that is resting in the heart and soul of a man. The place where no one can touch, hidden so carefully. A man is seeking a place to relax into his wound.

And what qualifies a woman to have conviction in her claim?

A woman must stand in her own true power of honor and trust. There can be no wavering from this place. Because what a man knows is strength. Strength beyond physical, this is a deep inner spiritual truth that you are a true Goddess. You have gone through your own fiery hell of your fears. You too have walked in your own darkness and shed unconditional light to illuminate your own Divinity.

A woman must first find her own strength within, love, nurture and hold her own self.

It is not an easy task to claim a man, because you must first claim yourself. You must take full ownership of the powerful woman that you know you are. You must know your rightness and never waiver from this truth. Your man seeks to be claimed by the Warrior Goddess within you, so that he may stand as the Warrior God that he is.

A full recognition that God resides in you both. And with this truth, the Vertical relationship can accelerate and create a new energy of relationship. Bound in truth, destined for God.

—TARA

the moment

the moment I heard your voice it resonated into my being...righting it into alignment...I came home...it wasn't a message to give you, it was possibility and potential...deep ability to grow with the same values, passion and way forward...it was the belonging I feel and the way your body felt touching me...I slept deep in your arms... safe...I felt so safe with you I was able to explore my own pain... you're the one who had the answers I trusted, and the vision of life that matched perfectly...

This is what I feel...it's the reason why I feel you and you feel me, it's the explanation of why even when we are not together our growth is identical...

It's an unexplainable reason of "why"...logic doesn't come into play...

there has been passing attraction to others, that drug-like sensation...yet when I do the "math"...nothing compares to what we have...and nothing has pulled me into a false sense of wanting another — each experience has only been to choose you

Your love has shown me who I am, it has opened my heart and dissolved every barrier I had to love, including loving myself...

Our relationship pushed the edges of conditioning, fear, self-confidence ...it made us authentic and molded us into our true selves...there is nowhere to hide and no reason to...because I love every aspect of who you are...I see your truth and all the personalities that cover your truth... loving all of it...my desire and pleasure is loving and holding your greatness, your potential and the truth of who you are...as a reminder and reflection...to hold you so you can step into yourself...the deepest love and the deepest honor to hold and witness you...

Your essence sings of Divine passion, seeing this world and breathing in the love of its art, beauty and music...the way you light up in ecstasy and moved by the poetry of life...I love sharing life with you, tasting all of it in deep appreciation...breathing in the colors and with exquisite attention feeling every flavor...

Devastating doesn't even define what I feel now...gratitude for all of it, is lost in translation...and goodbye is most likely impossible...

The Rumi poem...

The minute I heard my first love story,
I started looking for you, not knowing
how blind that was

Lovers don't finally meet somewhere,
they're in each other all along.
    —Rumi

Chapter Seven
Transformation

The Eagle who soars...can only spread his wings when he knows he is God
—A.T.

A sound on the winds of time
And I search for Truth
Finding the wind can play its tricks…
Illusions are mastered in a perception of lies
I come to find that sight is unreal…for the mind beholds its own
    patterns
laid as tracks on an empty record
we believe its message
One can look with clear vision
If you step away from that Matrix
Only the bravest of souls can reach this shore
Time is the greatest of gifts and illusions
And we walk in pain, never knowing the door is so near
Beyond the frame of existence lays the Truth in all is glory
I come to you, not wanting of a need
In my purest of states
I have sought the way
Found in its glory a position so clear
I guide you, not into illusion…
One must pull the others
For that is the only journey in the end

A healing vision

It was difficult, my visualization did not want to let go...a few minutes had passed, some of the duct tape returned...my heart aching for this representation of myself, trapped, dirty and suffocating. Half the tape removed, I cut off the loose piece...I gently pulled back the corner of the tape from the opposite side of the mouth...warm water cloth nudged the sticky tape off...I applied Vaseline on the skin...soothing the rawness and the application of the greasy substance deterred the tape from reapplying...

I worked in this manner as my heart opened—as I would for my daughter, or any child...yet this was an aspect of myself buried deep in my subconscious...so the effect had a personal physical sensation...all of the moments that I had suffocated the truth of who I am, was wrapped into this moment of freedom...

...She was finally free. She wrapped her arms around me, for security, for connection, for deep longing and desire for love...I held her with all my might—in a promise never to let go...protection was the pact, unconditional love was the bond...

I cut off her ratty knotted hair and shaved her head...a bathtub appeared and I soaked her tenderly in the warm waters of deep emotion and waves of love...I was beginning to feel reborn...I clothed her in a soft cotton shirt—the kind that reminds me of my Beloved...a thicker white knit sweater and loose white pants...

I tucked her into a fluffy bed, with a large down comforter...she snuggled in tight...I told her she can rest now, she is safe and loved...I had to go, there are 3 more doors to attend to...

The Mind

I see so clearly "The Mind"…
It's an illusionary field…that is playing games only with itself…
Mind hurting Mind…
We are caught in the distortion of its reality….
as it plays its games and discloses distraction,
We pull away from The Truth…
Even thinking The Truth is "out there"…
The other day I saw a person praying to God…
They looked up,
I laughed…
Like God would ever be floating in the sky??
When the stillness becomes your essence, the ocean floats through you…
God never has to be found…

To My Lover

To my lover, who has outlived your usefulness…
No longer embraced by the darkness you exhume…
Covered in the reality that you no longer cure my heart.
I walk amongst the flowers now
Wondering why I ever listened to
The madness of the habitual rhythms
Another churning of the unwanted chatter
I turned around and disconnected you from a matrix of lies
Freeing my heart to fill me with another song
Different in the play of ecstasy, in the dance
Of a new era,
My mind, my body and my soul return to
Their truth
Finally held in Holiness
Seeking the new way to live
In the footsteps of a path unpaved
My vision returns from slumber… "Goodbye old friend"
For I shall see you no more… You are no longer my destiny,
My truth, or my way…
You are no longer the chatter of my mind that played games with
    my reality
Your effects have no grasp of my consciousness
And it is the end…
of who I used to call me.

Kali...(Unfinished)

Kali rises out of the fiery depths, from the burning passion in my
    pelvis
I am filled with wonder and awe for this brewing world
Time returns to bring us into the existence of our longing

Home (second draft)

I don't even know what I am searching for...
a home perhaps?
I feel I will never find it here
This planet is beautiful, but I still do not feel part of its people,
Such an odd feeling...
to hold energy
and to do the work that is needed to heal this place...
No one would ever understand,
so I am alone in my thoughts,
traveling from place to place...
Seeking a connection, that sometimes I feel will never come...
yet I know this is my destiny...
Sometimes I long for the time of the Gods...
We weren't as veiled as we are now.
The veil does help us to understand the condition here...
it keeps us from knowing our true self

Untitled

In the black waters of my stillness
Creation stirs amongst the void
A lighting strike intensely
Illuminates
It is I who surrenders when there is no more to say
For an awareness to occur,
It will have to come from the heart
it beats for the existence
Of a memory faded
Golden splendor of the dawn
Awakens a reality of the past
I am consumed by another day
My blood fresh with tears and she calls to me
You are no more
I surrender into this reality
If only just to say goodbye
Will you miss me in the darkness?
No longer there to hold your hand
I can feel your love whispering to my heart
I know in this place,
there is a truth held from long ago
She will remember and we will grasp the edges of eternity
To dance again
This time Holiness will take a new form
And time will create a new journey

Holy Again

The scent of your skin pluses in waves, crashing on the shores of my innocence...
Fragrance of sweet flowers, earthy roots and tender young grass...
Filling my body with an intensity of lustful desire
They cut a haunting memory deep into my soul
I come closer as I breathe you in...
My mouth hungry to taste your essence...
My wanting opens a sacred portal and I kiss your chest... As if I can taste your light
My longing was heightened...
When I bathed in the waters of abandoned limits...
Mirrored by silky blackness...
and I stepped out of my lost personality
I am the Goddess awakened,
Clicking rocks of a liberating vibration,
Once Cloaked in the illusion of humanness...
I wish to take off all pretenses
Exposing the rawness of who I Am
All is no more
Purity returns to the body
The heart pumping into newness of a breath...
I come into vibration and then form...
Stillness awaits as I breathe you in and rapture engulfs my being
My wanting is boundless now...
Innocence is an explosion of desire.
I melt into your essence and
My power returns... The birthright of remembering
Dripping in tears, gratitude enfolds,
I Am Holy again,
Your scent, an ancient clairvoyant awakening

Reborn

I feel reborn today
Washed in the waters of my own innocence
I call my heart my home
The wonder of newness touches my soft silky skin
A breath, fresh with life
And the road has no markings
Nothing caught between the spokes
Liberating thoughts caressing passion for the unknown
A smile lifts the veil, a knowing
Bows to my being
I have come far to sit in this place
No more betrayal of a way that does not serve
I stand in my brilliance
With a strength I barely recognize and yet know so deeply…
For it is I who uncovered it
I am the one who braved that murky existence
To find a treasure buried deep
The old patterns laid a path, I no longer use
I have placed those maps on an alter of honor…
Talents celebrated and skills revered
Now satiated by my own questing
I come down off the mountain
Reborn, alive in my existence
To dance what was once a dream
To swim in the unknown
My body quickened in delight
And a truth of the warrior flows
If you look carefully, my eyes will tell you a story…
Holding your heart

They will tell you of a hunger and a battle
You will remember your journey is the same...
And my radiance mirrors a truth that you have lost

Creation

A whisper of my heart beats a deafening existence
Filling space in an explosion of ecstasy
Rocking my foundation to the core of disbelief
It is I who have come from the stars
And you who will meld into the reality of Oneness
While each crescent moon reshapes the patterns of my soul
Cells will shatter and tone will become form
The Gods will know it is time to reconvene,
Once again in the quiet place of
Stillness
Silence is the pattern, illusion is a stream
And I will sit on the mountain of creation
Listening to the beat of my heart,
Knowing the soul whispers a song
Deep into rhythms beyond time
The way is clear...
    —TARA

PERU—2013 AFTER I HAD MY SAN PEDRO EXPERIENCE

Death

There are many levels of death
Just as there are many ways to live
In death there is no failure
This is the true success of transformation

A Holy Chime

The faint sounds of a holy chime…metal touching metal
lulling me into a dream…the memory of our embrace
The soft kisses reach deep into my soul finding a place hidden from
    me…I had left my life behind in search of your lips, your touch,
    and your solid embrace
It was the mind only keeping me separate
Longing for connection
One with my beloved…
I found God, in your eyes, in your voice, in your recognition of my soul
We grew together, as a tree rooting itself into the earth
The strong winds of doubt pulling at our faith
Nothing kept us apart
In your Glory I became whole…not because of you
It was God I was seeking
And in our Love I found it all
Oneness truly resting in my heart

In The Arms of my Divine

Today I sleep in stillness
Resting in the arms of my Divine
I cannot shake the echoes of my mind
Nor can I soothe the untamed storm
That calls to my awakening
The mind will play its tricks
I once again lay
In the path of the warrior
Forgotten in the wave that crashes
On the jagged shores of my mind
Whispering to my soul,
"It's all a lie, can't you see what they are doing?"
I have come so far in my quest
To the knowing,
There is no quest
The quester is an illusion
The seeker and the warrior
Are an illusion as well
The only place to hold the Nothing,
Where there is strength enough
To form a container of this formless vapor
Is my beloved Divine
For this Beloved knows the illusions of my mind
And the longing of my heart
I am awakened
I seek no more for there are
No answers
Only truth in what I see

Ark of the Covenant

Ye shall remember unto this day
That God has made His promise to all men throughout all time…
His word is the word of words…
And you shall abide, not through fear and dishonor
Through the love and loyalty that comes unto you and it shall be
 written…
For ye who bestows his gaze upon me shall forever it be etched into
 his heart
The Ark of this Covenant shall forever remain…

ACT IV

Chapter Eight
The End

And in the end
The world is but a whisper
Finding its way to Truth
From the edges cast
A brilliant light
Fading out a silent scream for the savior…
And time folded its layers unto itself
A silvery death…returns home

Epilogue

Of Gods and Goddesses

The Gods and Goddesses came back to Earth
Slumbering within their own turmoil,
beseech thee..
"My Lord, what have we done to deserve such punishment"

God was quiet, as he knew, if the knowledge was not veiled, his
    children would never learn
And one by one, each God veiled from the truth, would encounter
    each other
Sensing a recognition, yet not knowing what they felt
The Ego came through… Twisting the reality felt through the heart,
Distorted through the mind…
In silence, longing for connection, they would never meet

Shrouded in their own significance they would never sense God
    standing in the path…

Mirrored reflections of the truth teased the Gods,
Dancing with a sense of purpose…
Posed to become a knowing within…
Waiting for recognition to settle into their core

One by one the heart of every God opened…
Experience rained upon their faces as they greeted each other…
By beauty and Grace
Reverence for who they had become,
each step lead the way for a new Earth to emerge

Time became a thing of the past…
The glory of the Gods revived all that was lost

Mighty and strong the Gods lifted one another and peace drifted
    into the hearts of man

Chapter Nine
The Final Beginning

Sat, Chit, Ananda

I Am, Existence, Consciousness, Bliss
I no longer need anything to keep me withholding...
I need nothing to keep me from connection...
I am no longer ashamed of my nature,
I trust myself and my love...
I want to receive purely, I want to give purely...
What came to me this morning was I have had many lovers...
There was great power in this...
Then I heard a voice talking...
"Take your rightful place at the head, you come before them"...
There is a powerful Divinely Feminine woman speaking...
She courses through me,
claims me and speaks through poem...

She is One with all
there is no fear
Only great power to wield as she wills...
She holds a Mastery of the laws of the universe,
She knows the secrets withheld from man...
She understands the balance of light and dark...
there is no importance held in each realm

Unconditional love guides her way beyond the need for a definition...
She transmits the Grace of God into those who can't remember who they are

I am the force of nature, the transmission of the Divine

I hold the destiny of my being in the embrace of surrender, mighty and enduring
She is the I who has shed her pain and suffering and has remembered she is God

Sri Yantra

I once met a man. We watched the sunset together at the Santa Monica Beach. He told me, "This," he pointed towards Los Angeles, "was thoughts having sex," and he went on, "it only takes the sun three minutes to fully set once it hits the horizon." He seemed so proud of this, as if he was the one who created the event. Then he told me, "You are stardust of the most exalted kind." I believed him. He never said it, yet I am pretty sure he is God.
—Tara

The symbol in this book is the Sri Yantra, one of the oldest geometric symbols known to man. This symbol is an ancient technology used to shift one into higher states of consciousness. Within the symbol is all of the created universe, as above, so below, within it a perfect ratio of 3.14, PI; and is a representation of the primordial sound, Aum.

"You realize the importance of tuning into a particular vibratory rate in order to elevate the mind and body from its lower, less ideal states, such as those of sickness and depression. You need not suffer from these states of mind. They

are illusions of the first class, and many of us have had them for so long that we forget that our natural state is one of joy, vibrant health and, bliss."
—Unknown

This book is dedicated to Humanity, to the evolutionary process of living in high states of consciousness. This is the next phase or Age of Humanity. Transformation starts within a dark night of the soul and moves through relationships, with others and self. Finally, resting our consciousness into the Truth of Oneness. A place we never really left, only an illusion that we were something else. No one knows for sure why or how or when, yet eventually one comes home.
—A.T. Sahota

www.ingramcontent.com/pod-product-compliance
Lightning Source LLC
Chambersburg PA
CBHW020540080526
44583CB00013B/925